MW01167071

Meet with Me

Meribeth Schierbeek

iUniverse, Inc.
New York   Bloomington

Copyright © 2009 by Meribeth Schierbeek

All rights reserved. No part of this book may be used or reproduced by any means, graphic, electronic, or mechanical, including photocopying, recording, taping or by any information storage retrieval system without the written permission of the publisher except in the case of brief quotations embodied in critical articles and reviews.

The views expressed in this work are solely those of the author and do not necessarily reflect the views of the publisher, and the publisher hereby disclaims any responsibility for them.

iUniverse books may be ordered through booksellers or by contacting:

iUniverse
1663 Liberty Drive
Bloomington, IN 47403
www.iuniverse.com
1-800-Authors (1-800-288-4677)

Because of the dynamic nature of the Internet, any Web addresses or links contained in this book may have changed since publication and may no longer be valid. The views expressed in this work are solely those of the author and do not necessarily reflect the views of the publisher, and the publisher hereby disclaims any responsibility for them.

ISBN: 978-1-4401-2866-0 (sc)
ISBN: 978-1-4401-2867-7 (ebook)

Printed in the United States of America

iUniverse rev. date: 04/01/2009

Dear Followers of His Word,

God's words to Moses were, "Be ready in the morning and then come up on Mount Sinai. Present yourself to me there on top of the mountain." Exodus 34:2

These words are for you and me, as well as Moses. The Bible was given to us. Each word in it is God's story for those who desire to follow Him, and live daily seeking Him and His direction, and hearing Him say, "Be strong and courageous."

This journal is just a tool for you to find a place to start in God's Word! It is 365 days of God's Word from Genesis to Revelation—the beginning to the end. We need daily manna to be able to survive and thrive spiritually in this world. Some of us do not know where to start in the Bible. It may be hard to know what God is telling YOU from a simple story about Jonah, or Noah, or David. You may have heard these childhood stories so many times, BUT God is speaking to you personally. The daily questions are to get you thinking about what His Word could be saying to you. Please use other parts of scripture to help you answer these questions. I used the NIV for this study and you will find that version easiest when answering the questions.

I want you to take Isaiah 55:11 as a promise from God: "My word will not return to me empty, but will accomplish *what I desire* and achieve the purpose for which *I sent it.*" Moses had to obey and walk up that mountain to be with God. My desire for you, and this tool in your hand, is to get up each morning; imagine God asking you, and waiting for you to come up to His mountain to meet with Him. Don't miss this special time waiting for you. **Begin with prayer!!** Ask God to reveal what He wants you to know through the scriptures, just for the day. Slow down; take time to read His Word, and use the questions to help you think about God and what He wants for you personally.

Your scripture and journal are in one book, so later you can look back and see where you were in His Word, the circumstances you were facing, and how God spoke to you. I left some space for prayers and journaling at the end. I pray this book may be just a spring board for you to get into God's Word. Our lives are so full of "good" things to do and be involved in; yet, if we are neglecting His Word, we will continue to wander in our purpose in the "best" life He gave us.

I look forward to hearing from you as you discover how full God's Word is, and what His purpose is for you personally.

Meribeth Schierbeek

justfollowtheword.com

Genesis 1-2:3

Who made all things?

How did God make all things?

What do your kind words do? What do your mean words do?

Write down all you can remember about the 7 days of creation.

What is your favorite day of creation and why?

Genesis 2:4-3

Look in Genesis 2:9, what was in the garden?

What is the one thing God told them not to do? Which verse tells you this?

Who tempted Eve with the fruit?

How did Adam and Eve feel when they sinned? How do you feel when you choose to sin?

What sin(s) is/are a temptation to you? Are you willing to ask for help?

Genesis 6-8

Why did God send the flood and why did God choose Noah?

Did Noah build it exactly as God told him? What verse tells you this?

Do you do exactly what God or those above you tell you to do? Why or why not?

God made a promise in 9:15 – What was it?

Does God always keep his promises?

Genesis 11:1-9

Why was it called the tower of Babel?

Did God tell them to build the tower? Why did they want to build it?

Can we know what God wants us to do without reading the Bible and talking to him?

What did God do in verse 8?

Where can you go (scatter) to share Christ, and what would you tell people about him?

Genesis 12

What did God say to Abram?

Did Abram listen to God? 12:4

What would you take on a trip, if you thought you wouldn't come back?

What happened because Abram lied to God?

Can bad things happen because you lie – Can you remember anything that has happened to you because of a lie? Will you share how it affected your life?

Genesis 13

What did Abram do when he wondered what he should do?

What do you do when you don't know what action to take?

Do you take time to read your Bible everyday? Why or why not?

Was Abram blessed because he loved and obeyed God?

Sometimes, blessing doesn't mean having "things." It might mean love from your family, health, patience in a trial. Can you name some blessings that God has given you?

Genesis 13:12–14

What city did Lot camp near? Was this a good or bad city?

Where are you camping that is bad? What places are you camping that are good?

What do you choose to read, watch or do? Are you choosing Lot's path or Abram's path?

Where will you choose not to go, watch or read this week?

Genesis 18:1-15 and 21

How did Abraham welcome the messengers from God?

How do you make people feel welcome?

What news did they give Abraham? What did Sarah do when she heard this news?

Would you believe if you were as old as Abraham? Do you believe the impossible for your own life?

Is anything impossible for God? What seems impossible for God to do in your life or your families' life right now?

Genesis 24

Where did Isaac send his servant to find a wife for Jacob?

Where do you go to find friends or mates?

What did Abraham's servant do when he needed help to find her?
Verse 12

Did God answer quickly? Does he always answer quickly?

What does the servant do when he finds Rebekah? Verse 26

What should we do when God answers prayer? What is one thing
you can thank him for right now?

Genesis 27

Whose idea was it to trick Isaac? Verse 5

Did Jacob not "want" to trick his dad or was he just "scared" he would get caught?

What makes you choose the "right" thing to do? How do your choices affect your future?

Would you trade knowing God for food or more material things? Think on this one for awhile...

How did Esau react when he realized his blessing was gone – taken from him? 27:34

Genesis 27:41–28:9

What did Esau hold against Jacob? 27:41 Did he hurt himself more, or Jacob, by holding this against him?

Esau had hate in his heart – What did hate cause him to do in 28:8-9?

Do you have hate in your heart? Will you ask God to reveal why, and choose to forgive as Christ forgave you? What action will you take this week to forgive someone?

Genesis 28:10-22

Read verses 13-15 again – How does that promise God gave Jacob encourage you?

What did Jacob do with the stone he slept on? Verse 18.

What can you give God to show your thankfulness? Verse 22.

Do you give with "I have to" attitude, or "I get to" attitude?

Genesis 29

What did Jacob ask for from Laban?

How did Laban trick Jacob?   Does this trickery sound familiar?

Who did Jacob trick early in his life? Gen 27:35-36.

What did Jacob have to do to earn Rachel? Verse 27

Can you earn forgiveness? Can you earn salvation?

What have been some consequences in your life for good choices?
Bad choices?

Genesis 32-33:4

What would you think if you heard Jacob was coming with 400 men?

What do you do when you are afraid? Do you remember what Jacob did? 32:9

How do you feel when you are forgiven or when you forgive someone?

What does it mean to you that Jesus took all your sins on himself and bore the cross for you? Do you hate your sin? Do you struggle against it daily? Do you journey alone or with God?

Genesis 37

In verse 5 Joseph tells his brothers about his dream – was that wise to tell them?

How did his brothers feel and what did they do?

Has someone ever told you about something special they got and **you** became jealous?

How did God use the bad in Joseph's life and make good out of it?

Has God ever used hard times in your life and made good from them?

Genesis 39

Look at 39:2 – Was God with Joseph?

What ability did God give to Joseph to help the king? Verse 8

Where do you find help in your life?

Where did Joseph get his help from? Verse 16

God gives us all talents/gifts/abilities – What are some of yours? How are you using them to give God glory?

Genesis 39:23-41

Did the cupbearer remember Joseph?

Does God remember you in all the details of your life?

What did the dreams mean?

Did God use his ability/gift for good? How? 41:39-40

Does God's word always come true? What is one thing that the Old Testament said and came true in the New Testament?

Genesis 42-46

Did Joseph recognize his brothers and did Joseph's brothers recognize him? 42:7-8

Why did they think Joseph asked for their youngest brother? 42:21-22

When you choose a path, or decide on a certain action, are there always consequences?

Do your choices help or hurt people? What is one choice that helped and one that hurt someone?

Genesis 45

Was it hard for Joseph to wait all this time to say who he was?

Who did Joseph believe made this happen? 45:5-8

Read verse 24 – What could you learn for yourself from this verse?

In 47:11-12 what does it say about Joseph?

Exodus 1 and 2

What is one thing you remember about the story of Moses' birth?

God protected Moses – What is one way God protects you?

He had a plan for Moses – What is his plan for you?

Are you one of His children as Moses was?

Exodus 3

Where did God speak to Moses?

God was concerned about his people – What did he want Moses to do?

Do you sometimes not do what you are told to do?

Look at Exodus 4:13-14 – Was God angry that Moses had so many excuses?

What are your excuses that you make? Are excuses a sin?

Exodus 5-11

See if you can write the 10 plagues down without looking in the Bible?

Did Moses and Aaron obey? Do you think speaking to Pharaoh was an easy thing for them to do?

Has God ever asked hard things of you? What are some of them?

God sent plagues as punishment. Are we punished today when we disobey? Does God still love us?

Exodus 12:31–14:13

How did God lead his people out of Egypt? 13:21

How does God lead you today?

How did the Israelites feel when they saw Egyptians coming after them? 14:10

Read 14:13 and see Moses' firm faith.

How do you react when you are scared and don't like what is happening?

Is God sovereign (in control) or are you in control?

Exodus 13:17–14

What caused the water to part, God or the staff he put in the water?

What if Moses wouldn't have obeyed? How important is it for you to obey?

Did they know God was on the Israelites side? 14:25

Take a few minutes and sit quietly and imagine the miracle of dry land; crossing the Red Sea.

How are you like the Israelites who don't believe God will take care of each detail in your life? What detail are you waiting for God to answer in your life?

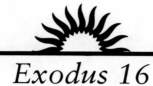

Exodus 16

How were the Israelites feeling in verse 3?

Do you complain about what is happening in your life sometimes?

Who are you really grumbling too? Verse 8

Did God give the Israelites all they needed?

How are you like the Israelites?

Exodus 17

What did the Israelites do when they were thirsty?

If you were Moses what would you want to do with the Israelites?

What did Moses do? Verse 4

What did Moses use to hit the rock and what came out?

Is it your abilities/gifts that make things happen or is it the power of God?

Exodus 20

Can you write the 10 commandments from memory?

Why do you think God gave them these rules?

Do you still need the 10 commandments in your life today? Why?

Will you thank him for providing clear instructions for your protection?

Exodus 24–40

Look at verse 1 – Where and when do you spend time alone with God?

Is God inviting you to spend time with him each day?

What gets in the way for you to spend time with God?

Think for a moment what it would be like for you to be able to literally spend 40 days with God as Moses did. Do you realize he never leaves you?

Exodus 32

Why do you think the Israelites made the golden calf? Verse 1 will help

Was Aaron leading in the way God wanted?

What idols could you possibly have in your life? (Remember an idol is anything that is more important than God.)

God sees everything – Does that make you feel safe or scared and why?

Re-read verses 34-35 Does God hate sin? Does he love His children?

Leviticus 1

Can you come to God anytime and anywhere?

Do you have to bring an animal, flour, oil or incense sacrifice?

Why do you not have to sacrifice animals before you come to God in prayer? I John 4:10

Whose life did your sin take?

Numbers 13

Challenge – Can you name any of the 12 tribes?

What did they find in the land while exploring? Verse 27

Are you excited when you see something you really want? What is something you really want and God would want too?

Look at the word "but" in verse 28 – Were they afraid?

Where are you saying "but" in your circumstances? Where will you choose to be courageous?

Numbers 20

Why did they need water? Verse 20

Do you complain when you are thirsty?

What did Moses and Aaron do in verse 6?

Honestly....What do you do when you have a need?

What did God tell them to do? Verse 8

Why do you think he hit the rock instead of speaking to it as God told him to do?

Numbers 22:21-23

Was Balaam doing what God asked?

What did the donkey see on the road?

Do you fight and fight to get your own way as Balaam did? Why?

Are there times when you try to go your own way and God puts road blocks up?

Look at verse 34 – Did Balaam repent and turn to God's ways? What do you need to turn away from to be on God's path?

Numbers 27:12-23

Moses got to look at the land of Canaan – Do you remember why he couldn't go in? (Numbers 20 will help)

Who did God tell Moses to send in his place? Did Moses' action have a consequence?

Has God chose you – Would you like to be Joshua replacing Moses? Why or why not?

Deuteronomy 3:21-29

What was Moses pleading to God about in verses 23-25?

When you have made a wrong choice, do you plead with God, your boss or your parents to take the consequences away?

Does God or another authority show mercy ALL the time?

Is God always good in His mercy and His justness? Can you and will you trust him with every person and circumstance in your life? Why or why not?

Deuteronomy 6:4-9

What does it mean for you to love God with all your heart, soul and strength?

What are ways you can write Gods commands on your door frames?

What do you talk about when you sit on the phone, or take a walk with a friend or go to bed at night? Does anything need to be brought to Jesus for forgiveness and a change in direction? Does any thanks or praise need to be given to God for the power to walk and talk as he would want you to?

Deuteronomy 7-8

Write down verse 6 – Are you set apart (holy) for God? How does your life show you are set apart for God?

Look at verse 6 again – Do you treat others or yourself as treasured possessions? How?

Deuteronomy 31

Who does Moses tell the Israelites will lead them across the Jordan?

Do you know that whatever happens to you; good or bad, God goes ahead of you? How does that make you feel?

Read verse 13 – What should children in your life learn and know? How are you teaching little ones in your life to do this?

Will you take the time to write verse 6 down and then memorize it today? What meaning does it have for you today?

Joshua 1

Read verses 6-9 again.

What does success mean to you? Write down whatever comes to mind "immediately."

Looking at that list you wrote down, does anything not line up with what God says is success?

What does meditate mean in verse 8?

Joshua 2

Do you remember the story of how Rahab protected God's men?

Read verses 10-11 again and try to think of someone that you know and it is evident that the power of God is with them and in them?

Does your heart melt/soften over the power and love of your God towards you? Why?

What did Rahab hang out her window to be saved? What color was it? Does the color have any significance?

Joshua 6-7

How many times did they march around the city?

Who was spared/saved that lived in the city?

When God tells you to do something "odd", do you listen and obey even when those around you don't understand?

Does God bless obedience? (Think of Rahab.) Where do you need to obey?

How have you been blessed by obedience?

Joshua 24:14-15

Does the enemy make serving/obeying seem undesirable sometimes? How?

Do you see others around you living for fun and stuff *only*? Do you sometimes feel jealous because you want Jesus **and** "stuff?"

Which will bring you more blessing; watching that new movie you just bought or inviting Grandpa and Grandma or some other person over to spend time with? Which one is easier?

Who will you serve and whose help do you need to do it?

Judges 6-7

Read 6:12-15 again.

You are a mighty warrior for God! What things can you do for Him?

As you think of your self as a mighty warrior strengthened by God to do His work....could anything stop you? What things stop you today?

How did Gideon and his men defeat the Midianites? (7:20-21 will help)

What are things we can do to defeat our enemies?

Judges 13

What was Samson's mother's reaction to the news of a baby and the directions of how to care for him? Verses 6-7

What would your reaction have been?

What did Samson's father ask in verse 12?

God speaks to us just like he did Sampson's parents. How are you taking time to listen?

Will you ask (and listen) to what God has for your life and work? What is he asking you today?

Judges 16

Where was Samson's strength?

Did Delilah keep persisting on finding out how she could get to Samson?

Where does the enemy keep persisting with you, wearing you down, so you give into the pressure? What is your greatest temptation?

Did Samson disobey God in telling Delilah about his strength?

Does God forgive and does he save his people when they turn back? Reread 16:28-29

Ruth 1

Why did Naomi and Elimelech leave Judah?

Was Moab a good place to go?

When things get hard in your life, do you look to "get away", maybe to wrong places?

Was Naomi angry at God? Verses 20-21

Did God use the "bad" for good in Ruth's life? How does the story end? Take time now to read to the end to see how God restores Ruth's life and gives her abundantly more!

I Samuel I

What did Hannah want really badly?

What did Hannah promise to give God?

What have you wanted and have been praying for? Could IT be used to glorify God?

Does God always answer prayer? Are you praying specifically so you know that God is answering?

I Samuel 3

How many times did God call Samuel?

Did Samuel know God yet? (Verse 7) Do you know God? Could he be calling to you?

What did Samuel say to God?

Are you listening for his voice or are you ignoring that voice so you can do what YOU want to do?

What does verse 19 mean with your name in it? Write it down somewhere where you can see it.

I Samuel 8

Did Samuel's sons walk in His ways?

Whose way are you walking in – God's or your own?

What did Israel want? Verse 5

Did they want what other nations have? Do you want other people have?

Did Samuel warn them they wouldn't like a king as other nations?

Are you content with what God gives you? What do you need that God has not given you?

I Samuel 9-10

Was Saul nice to look at? 9:2

Was Saul a good king or a bad king?

What is more important, how you look on the outside or how you look on the inside?

What are you more concerned about and why...be honest?

I Samuel 16

What did Samuel look for in a king?

What does God look for in leadership? 16:7-9

Are you small, large or not very smart?

Are you willing to let God lead where he chooses? What area in your life are you not willing to let God lead?

I Samuel 17

What are the Goliath's (big things) in your life?

Read verse 28 again – Do people try to insult *you* or make you feel little?

Look at verses 34-37 – Was David faithful in his work being a shepherd?

Did David try to be like someone else? Verse 39

Name 5 things that YOU can use to fight the enemy?

I Samuel 18-20

Did God give David a friend?

How do you treat your friends? Do you love them as you love yourself?

How do you put them first?

What can you protect your friends from?

Name the friends or people in your life that you are thankful for and say thanks to God for them?

I Samuel 24

Why did Saul want to harm David?

What sometimes causes you to hate someone?

Will you bring your jealousy before God and confess it?

What would you have done if you had the chance to kill Saul? Will you search your own heart and ask God if there is hate in your heart that needs to be cleansed?

II Samuel 11

Have you ever seen something and wanted it so badly?

Have you ever taken something that wasn't yours?

How did you feel trying to cover it up?

How did you feel when you confessed?

Was David full of sorrow over his sin? Does the consequences of your sin make you feel badly?

I Kings 17:1-5

How did God care for Elijah?

How does God care for you?

Does he give you all your wants or all your needs? Why?

I Kings 17

What do you do when someone asks for your "last" of something?

Read verse 13 – What do you think this means for your life?

Did she have enough for her family?

Did she doubt sometimes? Who did she go to when she had questions? Verses 17-18

Who do you go to when you doubt? Is Gods word truth and is it powerful? Verse 24

I Kings 18:16-21

Who brought trouble; Ahab or Elijah?

Reread verse 21 and ask yourself the same thing.

What makes you follow other things?

Do "things" truly satisfy or does only God satisfy?

How have you tried to get what you want, using all you have to get your way?

I Kings 19

Have you ever been afraid? When and Why?

What did Elijah do when he was afraid?

Elijah felt alone in doing Gods work. Does Satan want us to feel alone? Why?

Did God send help to Elijah and how does he send help to you?

I Kings 21

Whose vineyard did Ahab want?

What was Ahab sullen about in verse5?

Do you ever sulk when you don't get your way?

What did Ahab's wife Jezebel do?

When you do wrong, what is your attitude and what was Ahab's?
Verses 27-28

II Kings 2

Why did Elisha follow Elijah when he had told him to stay put?

Do you think Elisha wanted Elijah to be taken away?

What did Elisha want from Elijah before he left?

Was he sad when he left?

Did others understand his exit? Verses 5-18

When will we understand completely the things God does?

II Kings 4:1-7

Are you listening, obeying and trusting as the widow?

Are you asking for just a few opportunities to be a blessing or many?

God supplies our needs – How is God supplying your needs?

Would you have gone to your neighbors and asked for jars? What would you do?

II Kings 4:8-37

How can you be hospitable to servants of God? Verses 8-10 may help

How did God bless her in verses 15-16?

Where/who did her family go to when there was trouble?

Did she tell everyone she met? Verses 26-27

Did God answer the prayer of Elisha?

II Kings 5

Why did Naaman not want to wash in the Jordan?

Would he have been healed if he did not wash in the Jordan?

How important is obedience? Where do you need to obey?

II Kings 11

Who was put in to hiding in verse 3 to be protected?

Who are people in your life that protect you?

Is it always "fun" to be protected?

What happened in verse 12?

What special purpose could you be being protected for?

II Kings 17

Why was Israel exiled? Verses 7, 9b, 12 and 15 will help.

Look at verse 15 again – Are you imitating someone instead of being who God made you to be?

What are some ways that you imitate others? Are you afraid of being yourself? Why?

What would you act like if you listened to who God through the scriptures tells you to be? Are you seeking daily to live (not act) as God calls you to be?

II Kings 22

How old was Joash when he became king?

Is anyone ever too young to know, love and obey God?

Was he a good king? Why or Why not?

Read verse 2 and ask yourself if that could be said about you? Does it matter what people or God says about you? Why?

I Chronicles 1-9

Glance at each chapter.

Did you know that if you are a child of God your very own name is written down in heaven?

Think about that.....Is your name written down in heaven? Why?

I Chronicles 11:10-11

Ask yourself – Am I a strong support to Gods kingship?

How am I a strong support?

How am I a weak support?

Who is a strong support to you? Write the 1ˢᵗ person that comes to your mind.

I Chronicles 16:8-12

What are some wonderful acts that you can thank God for?

Who or what do you look to for strength and whose face do you seek?

Is it easy to seek God? What makes it hard? HE is always there, where are you?

I Chronicles 17:16-20

Read the question in verse 16 and ask yourself the same question?

Why did God choose you?

Are you amazed that God would choose you?

Read verses 16-27 and write down the things that showed how much David loved God?   Are you in love with Jesus?

I Chronicles

Scan the headings of each chapter and see if there is a job for each person to do.

In 28:5 who did God choose to build the temple?

Read 28:9-10 and write down the things you think are important and why they are? Where is your heart? Is it on things of this world or the next?

I Chronicles 29:10-20

Where does everything come from? Look up I Corinthians 4:7

How should we give? How do we sometimes give?

Who keeps your heart loyal?

Who gets the praise for all things? Do you give God praise or yourself?

II Chronicles 1:7-12

What did God say to Solomon?

If God told you to ask for anything – What would you ask for? What is the first thing that comes to your mind? Does it match what God would want for you?

Are you seeking Christ or self?

I Chronicles 3-7

Scan the chapters….but read Solomon's prayer.

Look at 7:11-22 – Was God pleased and how do you know that?

In 7:14 it says we are to humble ourselves – What does that mean for you?

See if you can put 7:14 to memory…

II Chronicles 10:1-14

Who did King Rehoboam ask for advice?

Who did he decide to listen to?

Where do you seek advice? Where should you look?

Who do you listen to when you seek advice? Why?

II Chronicles 12:1-12

Read verse 1 again and tell why Reheboam might have forgotten God and His ways?

In verse 6, you read that God is just - what does God is just mean?

Read verses 7 and 12 again and write down why God did not destroy them?

Where do you need to humble yourself in some part of your life?

II Chronicles 14:2-11

Was King Asa a good or bad king?

Why was he not at war with anyone for these years?

Has God given you rest?

Does the prayer in verse 11 sound like one that you say?

II Chronicles 20:5-13

Read this prayer and pick something that sticks out to you? Write it down.

Look at verse 12 – Where are they looking? Where do you look in times of trouble or good times? Do you look the same places in both good and bad times?

II Chronicles 23:11–21

Do you remember back to Joash; king at age 8 and protected?

Read verses 11-14 again – Do you think Athaliah was a nice person from reading this?

Honestly, how about you? Are you jealous a lot, are you power hungry, and is life all about you? Are you confessing it moment by moment and turning from your own desires?

II Chronicles 32:24-31

What did God bless Hezekiah with according to these verses? What has God given you the ability to have?

Look at verse 31 what did God do and why?

Do you think he told everyone his treasures were all from God?

Where do your treasures come from? Name your treasure(s)?

II Chronicles 34:1-8

Read verse 3 again and think about seeking God early in your own life....

If you are young – are you seeking him?

If you are old – when did you begin seeking him?

Ezra 1:1 and 5

What are some ways your heart has been moved? Who moves your heart or anyone's heart?

Do we sometimes think "experiences" move us? How so?

When you open God's word do you always ask God to open the eyes of your heart to see what he wants to show you?

Nehemiah 8

In verse 3 how did they listen when the Bible was read? How long did they read it?

Take a look at your attitude when the Bible is read – What is it like?

How often did they read the Bible in verse 18?

How often do you read yours? Is it on the "have to get it done so I look good list", or is it on the "I get to do this today because I am nothing without him list"?

Nehemiah 9

Does God hear in verse 9? Does God lead in verse 12?

Does God show and tell us great things in verses 14-15?

Do we sometimes not listen in verse 17? Is God compassionate in verses 19-20?

Does God warn us in verse 29? Is God just in verse 33?

Can we call on him in distress in verse 37?

What was the most important one of these to you today and why?

Esther

If you are familiar with the Bible can you recall the story of Esther?

In 4:14 it says that Esther might have been put in this position for such a time as this. Are you in any place or circumstance where you need to stand up or speak up? Where?

Will you choose to speak or be silent?

What did Esther do?

Job

Read Job 1 and 2 to familiarize yourself with what happened to Job.

What did he lose?

How did he react in the chapters that follow?

How did his wife react?

Read 23:1-12, 27:1-6 and 28:23, what was his attitude?

Read chapter 38 – Is your God powerful? Names some ways he is powerful according to scripture.

Psalms

Pick an old favorite or a new one to you and write all or part of it out and say why.

Proverbs

Do you have a favorite Proverb? Can you find one? Why is it a favorite?

Look at Proverbs 3:5-6. What does it mean to lean not on your own understanding?

Ecclesiastes

Read 3:1 and 3:11a

What time is it in your life right now? Teenager, single, married, dad, mom, grandma, working, retired….

Are you hurrying through and missing what he has for you NOW?

Song of Solomon 2:12-15

What are the foxes that ruin what God has planned for you, either with him, or with your husband/wife, or girlfriend/boyfriend?

What will you do to catch those foxes today?

Isaiah

Do you have a favorite chapter and verse in Isaiah? Will you write it down? If you don't have a favorite verse yet because you are new to God's word, ask God to give you one from Isaiah.

Look up 40:8 what is one thing that will stand forever?

Look up 55:11 what will never return empty?

Will you thank God for calling you and giving his son for you?

Jeremiah

Do you know and love any verses from Jeremiah? If so write them down.

Look up 29:11 what does God want to do for you?

When you think of prospering, what do you think of?

How might GOD want to prosper you?

Are Gods plans always good?

Lamentations

Read 3:22-27 and write down some things that are encouraging to you? Take some time and thank God for what he showed you today?

Ezekiel

Read 11:19 – What does a heart of stone look like? What does a heart of flesh look like?

Which one would you want?

Which one do you have?

Who changes a heart of stone to a heart of flesh?

Daniel 1

Do you remember what Daniel wouldn't do, what was it? 1:8

What did God give the four men in verse 17?

Do you think people wondered why they knew more than the magicians?

How can people wonder or see that you are different? What actions show you are different?

Daniel 3

If you have been a student of the Bible since you were little say one thing about the story that was new to you today...

Did God protect them?

Look at 3:16-18 — What was Daniel saying here? Think on these verses for awhile...

Would you or do you stand up for Gods ways? Why or why not?

Is it easy to stand alone? Who are your friends that will stand with you?

Daniel 6

Do you remember why Daniel was thrown into the Lions Den? If so, how?

Look at verses 3-5 and ask yourself why the men wanted to get Daniel into trouble?

Are you content how God made you? What has he blessed you with?

Did Daniel keep doing what God put in his heart? Will you?

Hosea 11:3

Read the verse and ask yourself two questions:

Do you know that God is the reason you are in the land of plenty? (Blessing)

Do you know he saved you? Have you thanked him for His son, the only thing you REALLY need?

What is one thought from this verse you will take with you throughout your day?

Joel 2:13

Does God want our gifts, service or our hearts? Which of these three is easier to give?

Say the 1ˢᵗ thing in your mind when asked this question…

…Is God compassionate or vengeful?

Why does he love to give grace to his people?

Why does he punish disobedience?

Amos 4:13

Read the verse again and write some things that God does?

What amazes you the most from this verse?

Obadiah 15

What deeds have you done that will return to you and bless you?

What are the deeds that you are sorry for and will come back to hurt you possibly?

Has God put anyone on your mind you need to go to and seek forgiveness? If so, will you go this week?

Jonah

Would you have wanted to go to Nineveh?

Did Jonah repent?

Did he go?

Are you quick to obey or quick to run the other way?

What was Jonah's attitude when Nineveh repented?

What is your attitude when someone is blessed undeservingly?

Micah 6:8

How do you walk humbly with God?

Do you love to show mercy? What are some ways you have been shown mercy recently?

Are you always fair/just?

Who is always just?

Nahum 1:7

What is a refuge?

Where do you go when you are in trouble?

Who/what do you trust in? Why?

Habakkuk 3:17-18

If you had no material blessings could you still say verse 18 with Habakkuk?

If you had no food could you say verse 18 with Habakkuk?

Why was Habakkuk able to be joyful? Why can you be joyful?

Zephaniah 3:16-17

In verse 3:17 there are three "He will" statements that show you what God will do. Write the three statements below.

...

...

...

Which one makes you joyful today and why?

Haggai 2:4-5

Who is with you while you work?

Do you ever not want to work? Why?

Who are you working for, God or yourself?

Where are you weak and need to be strong today? Are you asking for God's strength or trying it on your own?

Zechariah 4:6

How do all things happen?

If God's spirit causes all things to happen and not my might or power, can you just sit back and relax? Do you have a responsibility and what is it?

Read the last chapter of the OT talking about the future of Jerusalem and say one thing that excites you about it?

Malachi 2:17

How did they weary the Lord?

How does the world's way of thinking weary the Lord?

Does God say people who do evil are good? Does the world imply this sometimes, how?

Matthew 1

Who told Mary she was going to have a baby?

Who told Joseph?

Did Mary and Joseph believe?

What would you do with that unimaginable news? Do you believe the impossible?

Matthew 2

Where was Jesus born?

Why do you think he was born there?

Who came to visit him?

What did they bring?

What do you bring when you come to worship Jesus?

Matthew 2:13-23

Who didn't like Jesus?

Why didn't he like Jesus?

Why do you not like "some" people?

Did God protect Jesus and His family?

How has God protected you in big and small ways?

Matthew 3

Can you remember anything about John or his work?

What was his job or whose way was he to prepare?

How does your life show people the way? What are ways that your life might mislead people who are watching you?

Matthew 3:13-17

Look at Matthew 3:16 – What happened when Jesus was baptized?

When were you baptized and why?

Matthew 4:1-11

How many times was Jesus tempted? Can you name the ways?

What kinds of things tempt you?

How does that make you feel knowing Jesus knows what it is like to be tempted?

Is it a sin to be tempted?

Matthew 4:18

Can you name the 12 disciples?

Are you his disciple, if so how do you know?

Is there anything that scares you out of being a disciple of Jesus? What is it? Will you give that over to God so he can take care of that fear?

Matthew 4:23-25

Where did Jesus go to heal?

Do lots of people come to him to be healed physically or spiritually?

Which one do you come for?

Will he always answer?

Matthew 5:1-12

Take a few moments and try to remember one of the beatitudes and write it below.

In 5:12 what does it tell you to do?

Matthew 5:17-20

What does verse 18 tell you about the Law?

Why do we need the Law?

Which of the Laws have you kept completely? Does it matter if you have kept 9 and broke 1?

Matthew 5:13-16

What does a little salt do to the flavor of food?

How are you being salt with your friends?

Are you a light on a hill or a light under a bowl?

Do others see you being salt and light? Who do you want to get the praise for your actions?

Matthew 5:21-26

In what ways do you murder?

Can you worship God and be angry at a friend? Verses 23-24 might help.

Will you take time to ask God to forgive you for the ways you murder?

Matthew 5:38-48

Whose help do you need to love your enemies?

How well do you love others in your **own** power?

Write down one person who is hard to love for you and ask God to give you his love for that person. Take action today on loving this person and see how God can work through you.

Matthew 6:1-4

Do you tell everyone about your giving and doing?

Do you keep it between you and God?

Where is your reward when you give and do in secret? Where is your reward if you give and do in public?

Do you find yourself liking that instant reward or patiently waiting for God to reward? Why?

Matthew 6:5-13

Is praying hard for you? Why?

Are you praying to be heard or to spend time alone with your Lord?

What is your attitude in prayer?

Matthew 6:19-24

Are all "things" on this earth bad?

Where does God want your treasure to be stored?

Ask God to reveal to you where your treasures are and see if they are what God desires for you.

Matthew 6:25-34

What is the 1st thing you think of each morning?

What keeps you awake at night?

Read verse 27 again and write down how worrying can help?

Whose kingdom is 1st in your life?

Matthew 7:13-14

How do you know if you are on the narrow path or the wide path?

Is the wide path easy or hard?

Who is the gate?

What other ways do you try to get into the pen?

Are you in the pen? How did you enter?

Matthew 7:15-23

Can you recognize a Christian? How?

Why does God want a relationship with you?

Can we do many good things and still not know God?

Do YOU know him or just do good things for him hoping to get his approval?

Matthew 8:23-27

Look at verse 23 – Have you followed Jesus into the boat? Are you letting him lead?

What storms are you in a that Jesus lead you into?

What storms are you in that were caused by following your own desires?

How will you get back in the boat with Jesus so he can take control of the storms in your life?

Matthew 9:1-8

Would you or do you bring your friends to God in prayer?

When Jesus healed the man what did he do?

What does Jesus desire from you when he heals you either emotionally, spiritually, or physically?

Matthew 9:35-37

Do you know the shepherd? What are some of the ways you know he cares for you?

What do these verses mean for you today?

Matthew 10

Will everyone be accepting of you or the message you bring?

Read verse 27 and ask yourself if you are listening/hearing and then telling?

What are you more important than?

How do you lose your life and then find it?

Matthew 11:28-30

Are you weary and coming to Jesus for rest? Why are you weary? What does rest look like for you?

What is God like in verse 29 and what does God want us to do?

Are you yoked with Jesus?

Matthew 12:36-37

What do your words look like or sound like?

Will you take some time and ask God to show you what your words look like? Will you thank him for the good words and confess the bad words?

Examine your heart – This is where the words you speak come from. Why do you use the words you do; good or bad ones?

Matthew 13

Do you remember the 4 different soils? Name them if you can?

Which one are you?

Are you different soils at different times? Why?

Matthew 13:24-30, 36-43

Are you wheat or weeds?

Who sowed the weeds?

Who sowed the wheat?

What happens at harvest time? Where will you be when the harvest time comes?

Matthew 13:31-35

Does your faith seem small?

Do you need a little or a lot of faith according to this parable?

Whose branches are you perching on? What are some ways your faith is growing?

Matthew 13:44-46

Is Gods word and being His chosen your treasure/pearl?

If you have grown up in a Christian home have you taken it for granted? If so, how? Name some things you are thankful for.

What are you doing to take care of your treasure?

Matthew 15:1-20

Read verse 8 - Do your heart and your lips match?

What really makes a man unclean? Verses 10-11

Have you been trying to clean the outside of you by yourself – are you tired?

Will you ask God to clean you from the inside so what comes out is clean?

Matthew 15:29-39

Read verse 36 – Does he do the same with the 5,000 as he does with these 4,000?

Who took the food and fed the people?

How are you taking what you have been feeding on and giving it to those who are hungry around you?

Matthew 16:1-12

Faith or signs, verses 1-4 – Are you walking by faith or standing waiting for yet another sign?

Rituals or active faith, verses 5-12 – Are you using and giving what God has given you, or are you going through the motions doing your own thing?

Are you listening to that still small voice of the Holy Spirit? What are ways you hear him speaking? What could he be asking you to do today?

Matthew 16:13-20

Look at verse 15 – Write down who YOU say Jesus is?

Will you ask God to reveal more of who he is to you – verse 17?

Matthew 16:21-28

What 3 things did Jesus tell his disciples to do?

What do those 3 things mean in your life personally?

Matthew 17:1-13

Imagine yourself in verse 2, what are your thoughts?

Would you be Peter asking to build shelters so you could stay together?

God speaks to them in verse 5 – What does he tell them to do with his son?

Does he ask you the same question – are you obeying?

Matthew 17:14-23

Why couldn't the disciples drive the demon out?

God has all the power – Will you ask for a little more faith each day and courage to follow?

What is your circumstance in life today that needs more faith?

Matthew 18: 21-35

Is forgiveness easy or hard for you? Why?

Who do you need to forgive today? How will you do that this week?

Matthew 19:16-30

Are you looking for law abiding to save you or Gods' grace?

Are you holding anything back – not letting God use it for his glory?

Will you open your tightly clenched fist and see if he wants to take / use anything he has given you? What could you be holding on too tightly?

Matthew 20:1-16

Look at verse 12 – Do you sometimes feel the same way?

Are you looking at your walk as a Christian as a burden or hard work? Is there joy in it?

If it is hard work or a burden, could you be trying to do it by yourself, your own way, without a relationship with Christ?

Will you talk with him, walk with him and let him tell you are his child?

Do you believe you are his child? Why or why not?

Matthew 21:1-11

Read the story and try to picture being there? Write down what it would have been like to be there?

What are some of your thoughts or questions?

Look at verse 10 – Who do you say Jesus is?

Matthew 21:18-22

Who inspects your fruit? What does your fruit look like?

Is it possible to look good on the outside but be rotten on the inside? How?

Do you or your friends look good in front of others but not when no one is watching?

Does Jesus know our insides?

Where does Jesus say *you* need a clean up?

Matthew 21:28-31

Which one do you represent?

Do you follow through with your word?

Do you have a moment of "self" first then remember and obey?

What does Jesus want us to do when we **don't** want to obey?

Matthew 22:1-14

God invites you – what are some excuses today?

What would you have done – what are you doing with your invitation today?

Read verse 14 again – what do you think that verse means?

Matthew 22:34-40

How can you love God with all your soul, mind and strength? Is it possible by trying with all of your might?

Loving your neighbor as your self – Are you taking care of yourself so you can take care of others?

What would your life look like if you always loved God with all your heart, soul, mind and strength? When will life be perfect?

Matthew 23

Scan the whole chapter then look at verse 25.

Are you clean on the inside or the outside? Is one more important than the other?

What are the seven woes? Which one stands out to you and why?

Matthew 24:1-35

What are things you can do to help you stand firm to the end?

What will never pass away? Verse 35

Are you spending time in the one thing that will never pass away? If yes, how is it affecting your life?

Matthew 25:1-13

Do you have a lamp?

Where can you get oil to fill it?

When the ladies came late – What did Jesus say to them in verse 12?

How are you getting to know Jesus or are you just "assuming" you know him?

Are you ready for Jesus to return?

Matthew 25:14-30

Who has entrusted property to you? Verse 14

What are your talents? Write anything that God brings to your mind.

Look at verse 25 – What keeps you from using your talents?

Matthew 25:31-46

Are you hungry? – Who feeds you?

Are you needing clothes? – Who can clothe you?

Who in your life/path needs something (love, kindness, a listening ear?)

Are you feeding them or you looking the other way?

What could God be asking you to do for others today?

Matthew 26:6-13

Who anointed Jesus?

Are you afraid of what others will "think" if you follow what God is telling you to do?

What are some areas in your life that it is hard to follow God?

As Mary poured out perfume valued at more than 300 denarii's (which was nearly a year's wage,) what does that display about her priorities?

Examine where you spend your money, what does that tell you about your priorities?

Matthew 26:17-30

Did you notice how obedient the disciples were to Jesus? Is obedience still important today?

Jesus and Judas's names start and end the same – it is what is in the middle that matters. What is in your middle (heart)?

Matthew 26:36-46

Look at verse 39 – compare it to verse 42 – What are the differences you see?

How can you relate to sleeping as the disciples did? How can you NOT relate to sleeping as the disciples did?

Look at verse 41 – Do you think it is possible for YOU to betray Jesus? What does this verse say about the spirit and the body?

Why would you want to rely on your own strength when you know God has the power to keep you in perfect peace if you trust in him alone?

God will keep me in perfect peace if ~~the~~ I trust in Him alone.

Matthew 26:57-68

What do you do when you are insulted?

What did Christ do in verse 63?

How can you react the next time someone insults you? Will you ask God now to empower you to react as he "shows" you not as you "want" to?

But Jesus remained silent.

Matthew 26:69-75

How did Peter feel as he remembered Gods word to him?

What about your attitude toward sin – Does it look like Peters or Judas's? Why?

Matthew 27:11-26

Why did Pilate's wife warn him not to get involved?

Look at verse 24 – Are you trying to wash your hands from the responsibility of listening and walking with God?

Where are you compromising?

Matthew 27:45-61

Can you imagine for a moment being there and "believing" and yet watching Jesus die?

Why did Pilate have a guard secure the tomb?

Can anything stop what the will of God is?

Matthew 28:1-10

A violent earthquake opened the tomb – Has there been or is there now an earthquake in your own life that is opening your heart?

What are some things that you are concerned about right now in your life?

Look at verse 7 – Does Jesus go before us?

In verses 5 and 10 – What does Jesus say twice?

Matthew 28:16-20

What is the Great commission?

What do you do with your doubts?

Will you write them down and bring them to Jesus so Satan has no foothold in your life?

Mark 5:24-34

What did the woman think about Jesus in verses 27-28?

How soon was she healed?

Jesus looked for her – How did she come to him in verse 33?

As you look at the faith of this woman, what does your faith look like? Is it different than 5 years ago? Why?

What should your approach to Christ look like?

Mark 10:46-52

If Jesus was calling you, would you react as Bartimaeus did in verse 50?

What did he do after he was healed?

Do you know all of us need Jesus? He is here. Will you call out as Bartimaeus did in verse 47?

Will you follow and call on him even when others tell you to be quiet?

Mark 11:12-19

Why was Jesus angry?

Is anger ever right? Why or why not?

Mark 11:27-33

Where does your power come from?

Look at verses 31-33 – Why would they not commit to telling Jesus where they thought his power came from?

Where does all power and authority come from?

Where does this world think power comes from?

Who do you say Jesus is to you personally?

Mark 12:35-40

Who did the teachers say that David's son was?

What did Jesus tell them to look out for in verses 38-40?

Many people give different opinions. Where do you go to check things out?

Mark 12:41-44

What is the lesson that God wants to teach you through this story today?

In this story how did the majority of people give?

How did the widow give?

Do you know what it means to give sacrificially? What would it mean for you to give sacrificially?

Luke 1:39-45

Were Mary and Elizabeth excited to see each other? How do you know this according to scripture?

Why do you think they were so happy to get together?

Look at verse 45 – Do you believe what God says will be done?

Write down some promises that come to mind. Look some up in scripture.

Luke 2:41-42

Jesus was in the temple – Is your heart in the temple no matter "where" you are?

Why did Jesus want to be in the temple?

Why do want to be with Jesus everyday?

How much time do you spend with the Father? Why?

Luke 8:19-21

Are you a brother of Christ? How do you know?

Are you hearing AND obeying?

Will you ask for help in both hearing and obeying today?

Luke 10

What does it mean to be lambs among wolves?

Look at verses 5-16 – Who are people rejecting when they reject your message of God?

What does Jesus say to rejoice in?

Look at verse's 22-24 – Has God chose to reveal himself to you? Are you simply amazed by the gift of "getting" to see?

Luke 10:25-37

When are you the Good Samaritan – when you want to be or when God tells you to be?

What causes you to walk around someone who might need help?

Luke 10:38-42

Who is the busy, service minded one?

Who is the quiet one sitting at the feet of Jesus?

Can you do both? Which one is more important? Why?

Luke 11:1-13

Check out verse 1 – Do you have a special place you like to pray?

Are you bold in prayer?

What kinds of things do you ask seek and knock about?

What does God give you in verse 13?

What is the work of the Holy Spirit in your life? Does he live inside of you?

Luke 11:14-28

Look at verse 17 again – Who knew their thoughts?

Where did they think the power of Jesus came from?

In verses 21-22 it talks of power – who do you trust in, God or your own power? Why?

Look at verse 28. Who is blessed? Are you blessed according to what this verse says?

Luke 12:1-12

Who should you fear? Why and how?

How do you acknowledge who Jesus is in your life?

What are ways you disown Jesus in your life?

Who do you depend on to give you the words to say?

Luke 12:13-21

Is it bad to have possessions? When can it be bad? When is it good?

Combine verses 15 and 21; what is God trying to tell you about possessions and life with Christ?

Take a look at your wallet or checkbook. Where have you spent your last paycheck? Where are you storing your treasures, this earth or heaven?

What does your checkbook reveal?

Luke 12:22-34

After reading this story, ask yourself how God care's for your needs.

How do you care for others needs?

What does God want us to seek 1st?

Where is your treasure sometimes (honestly)? It may be in several places.

Luke 12:35-48

What kind of servant are you – What kind do you want to be?

How can you keep your lamp burning as in verse 35?

What has God entrusted you with? What is Jesus asking of you today?

Luke 12:49-53

What did Jesus do on this earth according to verse 51?

Will you stand for Gods word even when it causes division?

Are you listening to yourself or to God when it comes to being divided for the kingdom?

What are some areas in your life that God may ask you to be divided for His kingdom?

Example: Entertainment, music, friends, activities, books...

Luke 13:1-9

Where do your fingers point, out at others sin or inward at your own sinfulness?

Think about the fig tree…How do you resemble it?

Are you being fertilized or being cut down?

Who are you praying for that needs Christ 1st in their life? Yourself?

Do you need to repent and turn to God? What area in your life have you not let the light of Jesus into?

Luke 13:22-30

Have you ever wondered how many will be saved? Have you ever wondered "why me." Why am I so blessed?

What are ways you can know God personally? Do you know God?

In a world where everyone wants to be first, what does God say?

Where will you put others 1st today?

Luke 13:31-35

God desires to save His people – what verse shows that?

Imagine a hen gathering her chicks under her nest – How would that feel?

Are you willing to run under his wing (obedience,) or do you choose to do it your way (disobedience) - alone?

Is your house desolate? Have you said "Blessed is he who comes in the name of the Lord?"

Who in your daily life needs to be gathered under Christ? Do you?

Luke 14:1-14

What does your Sabbath look like?

Where do you choose to sit at a special event? Why?

Who are you inviting for dinner?

Read verse 11 again – Are you living humbly or exalting yourself?

Which is more fun – to life humbly or exalting yourself? Why?

Luke 14:15-24

What are the different excuses in this story?

How are you too busy? What are your excuses?

Are your excuses a sin?

Luke 14:25-35

What is your attitude in carrying your cross?

Where has God asked you to follow him trusting his will?

Does your will or Gods will come 1st? Honesty counts

When is it easy to choose Gods will over your own? When is it easy to choose your own will over Gods?

Luke 15:1-10

Read verse 2 again and ask yourself how or what do you mutter sometimes?

Are you rejoicing when people come to know God?

Look at verse 7 – 1 person repenting and 99 self righteous – Which group are you in?

Luke 15:11-31

If you know the story - write down what you remember and see what new things you learn as you read it again.

Who became in need and where did he go 1st?

Where did he go in verses 17-18?

Where do you go for safety and comfort?

How does God welcome you into his family when you seek him?

Luke 16:1-16

What kind of manager are you?

Who are you serving, God or money?

Are you seeking God to justify you or are you justifying yourself?

How do you struggle with serving God and not money?

Luke 16:19-31

Which one do you identify with?

Look at verse 26 – Are you or anyone you know waiting until it is too late?

Why do people wait?

Who did the rich man want to warn about Hell?

Who is in your life that shows you the way to life with Jesus? Are you listening or waiting? Why would you wait? Look up Psalm 91 and see the benefits of life with Christ.

Luke 17:1-10

How might you cause someone to sin?

How much faith do you need?

Who gives faith?

Are you looking for adoration for your duty (responsibility) as a Christian?

What should be your response according to verse 10?

Luke 17:11-19

How many were healed?

How many came back to say thank you?

How do you remember thankfulness in your life?

Will you take a moment right now and ask God who needs a thank you note from you?

Luke 18:1-8

What did the widow do?

What have you been persistent in prayer for?

How do you continue to be loyal and have faith?

Are you asking for Gods will or your will?

Look at verses 7-8 again – Will he find you having faith when he comes again?

Luke 18:15-16

What do you think receiving the kingdom of God like a child means?

Luke 19:1-10

How did Zacchaeus get to see Jesus?

How much effort do you put into spending time with God and his word? What stops you?

Did Jesus call him and ask to stay at his house?

What is your answer when Jesus calls you?

Did Zacchaeus repent and change his ways? Why?

Luke 24:13-35

Write down the parts or verses in this story that stick out to you.

What new things are you learning as you walk along in his word?

What has he revealed to you about himself as you travel through his word?

Luke 24:36-49

Why do you think they were frightened?

Why did they doubt? Do you ever doubt? What do you do with your doubt?

How did they finally understand? Verse 45

Do you try and try to understand the Bible? Will you simply ask him to open your heart and mind to him and help you understand?

Do you believe he can open your heart?

Luke 24:50

What do you think it would have been like to be there at the ascension?

Would you have gone home praising him as you returned to your day to day job?

Would you have left not believing?

How will you continue to praise God today?

John 1:1-18

What do you think "The word became flesh means"?

Do you recognize him in your day to day activities? How or Where?

Where do we receive one blessing after another?

Write down some blessings you have personally received.

John 1:43-51

How did God know Nathaniel?

How does God know you?

What did God ask Phillip?

Does he ask you the same thing today? How do you answer Him?

John 2

Why do you think Mary came to Jesus?

Do you come to Jesus knowing he has the power to do anything? If not, where are you going to with your questions and concerns?

What did the servants do in verses 7-8?

What causes you to obey?

John 3

What time of day did Nicodemus come to Jesus? Why do you think he came at that time?

What did he want to know?

Why do you think he couldn't understand?

Look at verse 21 again – How are we able to live by the light?

John 3:22-36

What was the crowd concerned about in verse 26?

Do you often concern yourself with who gets more?

What does verse 30 mean to you?

John 4:1-26

Does Jesus get tired?

Where do you go when you are tired?

Why do you think Jesus asked the woman for a drink?

Are you thirsty as the woman was in verse 15? Where are you going to quench your thirst?

What does it mean to worship in spirit and in truth?

John 4:39-42

Do you believe all the stories you hear?

What were a couple of reasons why they believed?

Why do you spend time hearing/reading Gods word?

What does Jesus mean to you? How could you tell others?

John 5:1-15

Did he want to get well?

Did Jesus tell him to take action?

What did Jesus mean in verse 14? How can you apply to this to your own life?

John 5:31-47

Look at verses 39-40 again – Do you have head knowledge and still not believe and love God?

In verses 41-44 whom did the people want praise from?

Who do you want praise from?

What does the word "believe" mean?

John 6:25-59

How is Jesus the Bread of life?

How are you feeding on the Bread of life?

John 6:60-71

Is it easy or hard to believe? What makes it easy and what makes it hard?

How are we able to come to God?

Can you say what Simon Peter said in verses 68-69?

Will you thank God for making you his very own?

John 7:1-13

Does he go secretly or with his disciples?

Can we come to God at any time or just at a certain time?

What keeps you from saying or doing things for God?

John 7:14-24

Where did Jesus get his learning/knowledge and also his words from?

Where do you choose to get your wisdom and words from?

Whose throne was he speaking for?

Look at verse 24 and write down what you judge by?

John 8:1-11

What is easier; looking at your own sins or someone else's?

Why do you think the older ones left first in verse 9?

What did Jesus say to the woman and what lesson is that for you today?

John 8:12-30

How or why did the people sound confused?

Why do you have questions and wonder sometimes?

Where do you go with your wondering and questions?

Look at verse 30 – Will you put your faith in him and trust him to give you the answers someday?

John 8:31-41

Are you a disciple, a descendant of Abraham?

What does Jesus say his disciples will do?

Look at your own actions – Which ones do you thank God for and which ones do you need to be convicted of and seek forgiveness?

John 8:42-47

How is your hearing?

What lies are you listening to? What truths are you listening to?

Will you ask God to open your ears so you can hear?

How will you humble yourself and listen?

Stop and think - has God ever had to humble you? How or why?

John 8:48-59

What does Jesus mean in verse 51?

Does everyone die?

Where do those who are Gods children go?

Where do those who are of "this world" go?

Will you live forever with Jesus? How can you know?

John 9:13-34

Did the man who was healed give them a lot of extra information?

Do you give just the facts or add "stuff" to your stories?

Why didn't the parents want to answer any questions?

When are you afraid of speaking up?

Will you commit to only speaking the truth as the blind man did?

John 9:35-41

Ask yourself the question in verse 35?

What does it tell you about him?

Can you see or are you blind to your own sin?

What does God want you to do with your sins? What do you do with yours?

John 10:1-21

Who is the Shepherd?

Who are the Sheep?

Who is the wolf?

Look at verse 4 – What does it mean to you that God goes before you?

Is there more than one gate?

Are you listening to the Shepherd call your name?

John 10:22-42

Are you living in a christian home/community/school?

Have you heard the stories in the Bible many times?

Do you find yourself believing and following God or choosing to question as the unbelieving Jews?

If you answered yes to question 1, how are your actions showing what you have learned or are learning? What areas need a little work? Can you do any "good" thing on your own without a relationship with Christ?

John 11:1-16

If your friend is in need would you go to a place of unrest to help him as Jesus did? Why or why not?

Where did Mary and Martha go in this time of need? Where do you go?

Look at verse 16 – will you follow Jesus no matter what people think or what lies ahead?

If God is for us who can be against us?

John 11:17-37

Where is Mary and where is Martha?

Each one has different gifts – What are yours?

John 11:38-43

Jesus gave them an action to do – what has he told you to do today or another day?

Are you afraid like Martha was in verse 39b?

Do you believe God will provide wherever and however he leads you?

Jesus takes off the bondage of Lazarus, what does he have to relieve you from today?

John 13:1-17

Why didn't Peter want his feet washed at first?

Did Peter want them washed after he knew why?

Are you washed – Where and how do you seek daily washing and cleansing from your sin?

Why would you let Jesus wash your feet?

John 14:1-4

What is one thing that encourages you in these verses and why?

John 14:5-14

How can you really know Jesus as it says in verse's 6-7?

What does he want of you?

John 14:15-31

How do you know the Holy Spirit lives in you?

Do you wear a "Christian" label with no obedience? Are you listening to the Holy Spirit, leading and guiding you? What do you do when you hear that still small voice giving you direction?

There is a promise in verse 21 – write down what it is.

John 15:1-17

How are you attached to the vine?

What happens to vines that are not attached?

What fruit are you bearing that will last?

John 15:18-27

Do you ever feel weird or disliked because you follow Jesus?

Would you rather be loved by the world or by Jesus?

How would life be easier at the present time – being loved by the world or loved by Jesus?

Do you remember Jesus was hated too?

John 16:5-16

Are you listening to the Holy Spirit – What has he prompted you to do lately?

Read verses 13-14 again and ask yourself what does the Holy Spirit do?

What are some reasons you do not hear the Holy Spirit sometimes?

John 16:17-33

Look at verses 17-18 – Who do you ask when you have questions you don't understand?

Did Jesus know their questions?

What was Jesus excited about? (Hint: It is in verse 33)

Will your time on this earth be trouble free? Why or why not?

John 17:1-5

Do you remember to pray for yourself?

What things do you ask God for about yourself?

What did Jesus tell God about in these 5 verses?

John 17:6-19

Do you pray for your friends? Who are your friends?

What kinds of things would you include from Jesus' prayer for your friends?

John 17:20-26

Do you pray for people you meet on the road/ school/work or just your friends?

What should you be praying for about the people who are in your path each day?

Is there someone in your heart/mind that does not show love in there outward actions? Will you commit to pray for them?

John 20:10-18

Would you have stayed as Mary did or would you have gone home?

Do you know Jesus knows your name personally and knows you better than anyone else?

What did Jesus tell Mary to do?

Who are you telling? Are your actions telling others who you belong to?

How are you able to have "good" actions?

John 20:19-23

Jesus sends them out in verse 21 – What does he give them to do the work?

Are you willing to let the Holy Spirit work in your life and go out as he prompts you to?

Does it sound exciting or scary to be a disciple? Why or why not?

Where could God possibly be sending you in small ways (example visiting a person in need, letting go of someone or thing...?)

John 20:24-31

Can you remember the main theme of this story? (verse 27 may help)

Have you or do you ever sound like Thomas in verse 25b?

Read the verse 25b again – How does it sound?

Is it hard for you to believe when you have not seen for yourself?

John 21:1-14

What do you do when you have had a bad day "fishing"?

Are you beginning each day asking God to be your guide?

Do you listen to God as he tells you to change direction?

Where have you listened to God and fished the other side of the boat and found success? Have you not listened and not fished the other side yet?

John 21:15-25

What does Jesus ask Peter to do 3 times?

Do you often say or think – what about him/her as Peter in verse 21?

Are you listening for what God wants YOU to do or are you wondering/complaining why ME, what about her?

In what area/time in your life have you said why me?

Being called by God to be his disciple is the highest blessing ever – will you or have you answered? What actions of faith are you taking since you know you have been called?

Acts 1:1-11

What question did they ask in verse 6?

Were they looking for their own kingdom to be restored?

Was Jesus' answer about this world, or the coming kingdom, that he will rein over forever?

Whose kingdom are you living for?

Look at verse 8 – What kind of witness are you for his kingdom?

Acts 1:12-26

Are you constantly in prayer in each decision you make? What do you ask God for daily?

What are some decisions you have to make each day?

Acts 2:1-13

What do you do when you are bewildered or utterly amazed as they were in verses 6-7?

Do you ask questions as in verse 12 or do you mock and make fun of an event as in verse 13?

Acts 2:14-41

What was the response of the people in verse 37 knowing they put Jesus to death?

What is your response to God's word? Is it a "so what" or a "what shall I do" attitude?

Does your action look like verses 38-41?

Do you talk of sin or repentance as Peter did in verse 38 in your church today? Why?

Acts 2:42-47

Is this what your neighborhood or community looks like? What about your neighborhood is different?

What are you devoted to?

Do you enjoy people as they did in verses 46-47a? How could this happen today?

What will you do this week to enjoy other believers?

Acts 3:1-10

What things do you expect to get from Jesus?

What did the beggar plan on getting from the disciples?

What are some promises to us from God?

Acts 3:11-26

Who/what do you have faith in? Verse 16

Read verses 17-19 again – Do you claim ignorance or repentance to the truth? How do you choose to ignore the truth some days?

Who was the 1st person God sent his servant to after he was raised?

Acts 4:1-22

What was the question the Sanhedrin asked and wanted to know?

How did Peter answer them – kindly or harshly?

How do you answer when you are asked a question?

Who is the most important person to obey? Who are the people you like to obey? Why?

Acts 4:23-31

What is the 1ˢᵗ thing the people did when they received news?

What is the 1ˢᵗ thing you do when you hear news?

What happened after they prayed?

Do you pray expectantly and believing? How has God answered prayers of your past?

Acts 4:32-37

Do you think they gave money to the poor in Bible times? Were there poor people in Bible times?

What would be the benefits of sharing your possessions?

What would be the benefits of not sharing?

Acts 5:1-11

God knows all – why do you hide things from him sometimes?

Do your choices look like Ananis and Sapphira's?

According to this story does God punish disobedience? Does he reward obedience?

Acts 5:12-16

Who are you bringing to God through prayer who needs Gods healing physically, emotionally or spiritually?

When do you take time to pray and spend time with those in need?

What stops you from spending time with those in need?

Acts 5:17-41

Who did the apostles obey?

Who does God give his Holy Spirit to?

Was life easy for the apostles?

What encouragement can you find in verses 38-39?

Acts 6:8-15

How did verse 8 describe Stephen? How would someone describe you?

In verse 10 it says it is impossible to stand against Gods power. So why would someone choose to try to go through life without asking God for HIS power to live for him each day?

Has someone ever lied about you? How did/do you react, and what is the correct way to act according to the Bible?

Acts 7

Stephen makes a bold call to repentance – what was the crowds reaction and what is yours?

How would you react if someone called you stiff necked as in verse 51? Was it true of them? Could you be stiff-necked in some places in your attitude?

Is your reaction like verses 59-60 to those who hate you because you love Jesus more than life?

Acts 8: 1-3

Are you one of the godly men that buried Jesus?

Are you like Saul who destroys the church?

Does God scatter people for a reason? Why would he scatter some?

Acts 8:9-25

What did Simon want to do in verses 18-19?

What is the only way to receive the Holy Spirit?

What do you think about Simon the Sorcerer? What does scripture say about him?

Acts 8:26-40

How are you listening to God's voice and following as Phillip did here?

Phillip explains the scriptures and what happens?

Do you or would you take time to read the scripture to yourself and others? Make a plan for it.

Phillip leaves – Does the eunuch stop believing?

Do you believe in God or just the person who delivers the message? Who are you following?

Acts 9:19b-31

Where did Saul begin to learn?

He tried to join the disciples in verse 26 – Why were they afraid of him?

Why would you be afraid of someone like Saul?

How did God protect Saul?

Acts 9:36-43

What do you do when you are wondering what to do?

What did Peter do after he sent everyone out of the room?

If you heard of healings like this one, would you be quick to believe?

Do you want physical/worldly healing only or spiritual healing and a closer walk with Christ?

Acts 10:1-8

What is Cornelius like?

Does this sound like anyone you know? Yourself?

When you know God is leading you, do you obey as Cornelius?

Do you think he understood before he obeyed?

When do you obey?

Acts 10:9-23

Do you ever wish God spoke to you as he did in the Bible?

If you belong to Jesus his Holy Spirit does speak to you – are you spending time praying as Peter did in verse 9?

What in Peter's vision jumps out to you or is new to you? Take this with you today.

Acts 10:23b-48

Does God show favoritism? Do you show favoritism?

Who does God accept? Who do you accept?

In verse 44 do you think they heard the message with their hearts or heads and why?

Acts 11:1-19

When someone needs some explanation, do you tell them or stay away?

What did Peter do in verse 4?

When they heard the truth what was there reaction?

Do you accept new people into your circle of friends? Is this easy or hard for you and why?

Acts 11:19-30

What was Barnabas like and what did he see in Antioch?

How could this describe you and what you see when you arrive in the places you go?

The 1st church was started here and the disciples were called christians…which word do you like better, disciples or christians and why?

Acts 12:1-19

What was the church doing while Peter was held in prison by a wicked king?

What do you do when there is a problem?

Look at verse 6 – why do you think Peter could sleep?

List some reasons Peter could have been scared to death?

Can you ask God for faith and expect him to answer?

Acts 12:19-25

Is God always just and fair?

Was Herod always just and fair?

Why did God strike Herod dead?

Do you praise God because you love him or fear him, or both?

Will God's will and his word continue to go forth? Why?

Acts 13:1-3

How did they send Barnabas and Saul out?

Who called them to this work?

What do you think about fasting and laying hands on?

Do you fast today? What are your reasons for or against fasting?

Acts 13:4-12

What is Satan's main job?

What are some ways he uses to get his job done?

Whose name is more powerful – Jesus or Satan's?

When you are faced with lies of Satan will you name the name of Jesus to combat lies with the truth?

Are you spending time in the truth so you know the truth and won't believe lies?

Acts 13:13-52

In verse 15 they gave encouragement, how are you encouraging people of God?

Is God merciful according to verse 18?

Does verse 22b describe you? Who is the message for in verse 26?

Read verses 38-41 again, will you perish or believe?

What happens when you stand for truth according to verse 45?

Many of us have heard the message over and over – Will you believe with action of the heart or will you wonder and perish?

Acts 14:1-7

What did Paul and Barnabas do and is this what you do?

How does God protect his people?

Acts 14:18-20

Look at verse 9 – Can others see your faith?

When God gives you direction, do you get to it, even if it is a little hard?

What happened to Paul in verse 19?

Do you gather around other Christians that have been hurt? Do you talk about them or go to them and offer yourself?

Acts 14:21-28

Is following God hard sometimes according to this passage?

Does God give grace, joy and rest as we follow him? How do you see that in this passage?

Why do you think Paul and Barnabas appointed Elders?

Why do you have Elders in your churches today?

Acts 15:1-35

Are outward signs or inward signs important?

Who chooses who will believe?

What yoke were they trying to put on the people?

How are we saved?

What does God ask them to do in verses 19-20?

Do your outward actions show your inward heart? "Actions speak louder than words."

Acts 15:36-41

Are disagreements always bad?

What happened from this disagreement?

Did Gods word go out further by this split – How?

When has a disagreement been a good thing in your life? What did you learn from it?

Acts 16:1-10

Are you growing in your walk with Jesus as these churches were growing?

What are ways we grow as Christians? What causes you to grow?

Acts 16:11-15

Lydia was already a worshipper of God, was she still learning and changing in verse 14?

Lydia's outward actions were good – no lying, cheating, gossiping … Do those actions alone make her a Christian?

Her and her household were baptized – Do you think she followed with her heart AND her actions? What makes you say that?

How about you – are you giving bits and pieces of your life only, or your whole self for God?

Acts 16:16-40

What happened when Paul commanded the evil spirit to come out of the girl?

Do conflict/problems come when you do what is right sometimes?

After Paul/Silas were beaten, what did they do?

What would you have done when you discovered that Paul and Silas were still there?

Do your actions make people wonder if you are a Christian?

Acts 17:1-9

Some believed and some were jealous?

Which one are you?

What things make you jealous? When will you be free from jealousy for good?

Acts 17:10-15

How did they receive the message?

How is your attitude in going to church to hear a message?

What did the Jews do when they heard the word was being taught in Berea?

Do you go wherever you can to learn more? Example; Bible Studies, Sunday school....

Whose help do we need in order to want to learn more about Jesus?

Acts 17:16-34

Did the people here understand?

What was the city full of?

What did they do with the news in verse 21 and 32?

Take some time and think about Jesus taking your sins and dying for you…What are your feelings or thoughts?

Acts 18:1-17

Do you show concern for those who are hurting?

What are ways you have helped or can think of to help? Will you take action this week?

What did Paul do every time he could to help others?

Acts 18:18-28

Who was Apollos?

Was he a smart man?

Did he think he knew it all or did he continue to learn?

Was he excited to tell the good news?

How are you continuing to learn? Where are you telling the good news? Are you keeping it to yourself?

Acts 19:1-22

Did God do extra ordinary miracles through Paul?

Why did the Jews want to do awesome miracles?

What happened to the Jews who used Gods power for their own glory?

Do we need to reverence/respect how we handle the power/talents/ gifts God gives us?

Acts 20:13-38

Did Paul go a lot of places?

What was his mission or purpose?

Was he afraid of what could happen if he followed?

Was he worried about getting "things" in his life?

Did he leave in tears, yet knowing God would watch over the ones he loved?

What can you learn from Paul today?

Acts 21:17-26

What was most important to the Jews?

Notice in verse 1 – Did the brothers receive Paul warmly?

How do you receive other believers or non-believers?

Did Paul abide by their customs or laws?

Are you following customs or God? Are you following friends or God?

Acts 21:27-22:29

Imagine yourself in verse 30 – How would you react knowing God is in control?

Paul takes the opportunity to speak – would you have?

Maybe you do not have a lot of words. Can you speak with your actions and not your words?

Paul tells of how God changed his heart and chose him...Is God changing you? What things are important in your life?

Acts 22:30–23:11

What did Paul call Ananias? What does that mean?

How are we to treat rulers/authorities according to verses 4-5?

The crowds are in an uproar…What does God say to Paul?

Are you walking in obedience to God in your life? If so, take Gods word to Paul for yourself?

How do these words to Paul encourage you?

Acts 24

Did Paul rant and rave about the false accusations against him?

How do you react when others accuse you falsely?

Look at verses 24-26 – Did Felix like hearing about Gods word? Why do you think he was afraid?

What did Felix want Paul to do and why?

Acts 25:1-22

Did Festus want to convict Paul?

Why do you think he sent Paul onto the next judge?

How about you – are you willing to recognize sin as sin, and right as right, or do you sit on the fence not willing to stand firm?

Is it easier for you to please man or God and why?

Will you confess your sins or justify your actions?

Acts 25:23–26:32

Paul tells his story again – Do you notice any new details?

Reread 26:12-23 what things stand out to you? As you read them write them down. Which ones can you use to encourage you in your own walk?

According to 26:28 does King Agrippa believe the gospel?

In verse 29 what does Paul want for him?

Paul was becoming more like Christ everyday, is that your desire for yourself also?

Acts 27:1-13

How did Paul warn them of what was ahead?

Did the centurion listen?

Who are the people in your life who tell you of what is ahead? Are you listening?

Some things happen because of disobedience, some happen so we can become more like Christ. Who is directing your ship, you or God?

Acts 27:13-26

Where are you letting storms or the winds carry you?

In the storms of life, have you thrown the things you need (God, His word and His people) overboard? What did they throw overboard?

Have you lost your courage or given up hope as in verse 20?

Have you run aground on some island – How are you seeking God's direction and gaining courage from him to stand?

Acts 27:27-44

Where do you see God's protection for Paul here?

Did Paul eat and give thanks in front of everyone?

How are you living out your thankfulness to all you live with? Do you hide your love and faith under a bushel at times, why?

Acts 28:1-10

How were they welcomed ashore? What are some ways for you to follow that direction?

What did the people expect to happen after the snake bite?

What did they think Paul was in verse 6?

How is it possible for you to welcome people, love enemies, and shake off people who want to hurt you? Can you do this in your own power?

Will you ask daily for a fresh filling of Gods' spirit? What action will you take knowing he will answer?

Acts 28:11-16

After three months of refreshment they boarded a ship with what on it? What would you think getting on a ship like this?

What did they find in verse 4?

What people/friends has God put in your life to help you seek him?

Did Paul thank God for what he gave him? Take some time to thank him now.

Acts 28:17-31

Do you have Paul's passion for telling others? How is it possible to tell others without saying a word?

Look at verse 23 and 31 – How can you get this excited about God and his word to share it with all you meet?

Do you try and try to get people to believe and love your God? Will everyone choose to love Him? Who makes it able (calls) for someone to believe?

Will you ask God for vision, hearing and a heart that sees, hears and wants to know him more personally each day? He will answer.

Romans 1:1-6

Can you put your name where Paul's is in verse 1?

What does it mean to be a servant of Christ for you personally?

What does it mean to be set apart?

Put your name in verses 5-6 where the we's and you's are – What do you like about putting your name here?

Did you know obedience comes from faith?

Romans 1:14-17

Why was Paul obligated to go to all with the gospel?

Can you say with Paul you are not ashamed of the gospel?

What is revealed in the gospel?

Do you live by faith or works? Which sounds easier and why?

Romans 1:18-32

Look at verses 21, 24, 26 and 28. Do you see that when you continue to sin refusing to seek him, God gives you over to what we keep chasing after? What are you chasing after?

What are some things in this part of scripture that you struggle with or that you see in your world of church, home, school and work?

Read verse 32 again and examine yourself – Are you continuing in sin or seeking him daily reaching out for his help to follow him?

Who or what are you approving of that is not in line with God's will for you? What will you do about it?

Romans 2:1-11

What does God base his judgment on? What do you base your judgment on?

What is it that leads us to repentance?

What is being stored up for you on the last day – God's wrath or mercy? Why?

Do you seek your own glory or God's glory?

Where do you show favoritism?

Romans 2:17-29

Are you teachable or unteachable? Do you tell others what to do, or do you learn along with others?

What do your actions say about who you are?

Does God want actual outward circumcision (acting), or circumcision of the heart (love)?

Which one do you have? Do you look good on the outside for others to see or are you walking humbly before God each day?

Why is it hard to walk humbly sometimes?

Romans 3:1-8

What advantages have you had in your life? Exp. Christian home, school, church….

How have you been entrusted with the Bible knowledge in your life?

Does *your sin* increase Gods glory or does a *sinner confessing* his sin bring God's glory?

Will your condemnation be deserved because you don't care if you continue in sin?

Why does your sin bother you?

Romans 3:9-20

Is anyone better than anyone else?

Where do you find yourself in verses 10-18? As you read that list, which ones do you struggle with? Will you talk to God about it; he is waiting for you each day?

We talk about being free from the law because of God's grace, what does verse 20 say about this?

Does the law help in showing you your helplessness and drive you to the cross for His mercy and His grace?

Check out the 10 commandments in Exodus 20 – Do you hate your sin enough to confess it, turn to the cross and seek Christ?

Romans 3:21-31

Where does your righteousness come from?

How do you sin and fall short everyday?

Can you boast or think highly of yourself because you keep all the laws and commandments? Why?

Do you realize your faith is a gift from God? Why would he give it to you? Can you ask for more faith?

Romans 4:1-12

Do you give a lot of advice – Do you talk a lot? What do you base your speech on – look at verse 3?

Look at verses 4-6 – Are you **working** for your righteousness? Are you tired yet?

Is God looking for outward obedience or inward *and* outward love and obedience?

How does your heart and actions match? Does your sinful nature sometimes fight against what you know is right?

Romans 4:13-25

Read verses 14-15 again – Do you think you should read the law frequently? Why or why not?

Abraham believed – think over his life…Does your faith believe against all circumstances, hoping in God's power and glory?

Do you honestly believe all things are possible with Christ? What are some impossible circumstances in your life right now?

Did Abraham waver in verse 20? Why?

Romans 5:1-11

Put your name in the we's in verses 1 and 2. Can you say this about yourself?

Does suffering make you more like Christ or has it make you bitter? Do you choose bitterness or Christ?

Did God die for you because you are a nice person?

How much more do you want to give God glory because of his amazing gift of life in and through his son? How will you give him praise today?

Romans 5:12-21

How did sin enter the world?

How did salvation come into the world?

Look at verses 18-19 – one man – one action – which man are you striving to follow?

Did sin enter easily? Did salvation enter easily?

Why is it so easy to choose sin over obeying sometimes? Can Satan make sin look good?

Romans 6:1-14

Look at verse 4 slowly – put this verse in your own words with meaning for your life?

Are you still a slave to sin not living in the power of Christ?

Did you know when you belong to Christ you have his power to choose not to sin?

Is sin still your master, do you keep trying to do all things without Christ?

What are things you have struggled with forever it seems? Whose power are you relying on with these struggles?

Romans 6:15-23

Are you a slave to sin or are you choosing obedience through Christ?

Which one leads to death which one leads to life?

How have you been set free to live in Christ power?

Benefits in this life are important when looking for a job - What are the benefits of a personal relationship with Christ in verse's 21-23?

Romans 7:7-25

Which commandment do you struggle with the most?

Read verses 7-12 again and write why the law is good?

Do you hate your sin? Has it become utterly sinful to you?

What is Paul saying in verses 14-23 about HIS ability to do good?

What does Paul say in verse 25? Who has the power to work in you and through you to do his good? How will you choose to obey today?

Romans 8:1-17

What is your mind controlled by? What are the things you think about most? Be honest God already knows

Does Gods spirit live in you? Read verses 1-2 putting your name where the "me" is? Is it true for you?

Are you a son of God – Are you a slave to fear or have a spirit of son ship? What do you fear most? Can God take this fear from you and will you choose to let him?

Romans 8:18-27

What are some things in your life that you are "suffering" with?
Don't think BIG things...

Are they worth comparing to what God promises you?

What do you hope for today and for eternity?

Do you wait eagerly yet patiently?

Is prayer hard, not knowing what to say? Why does verse 27
encourage you?

Romans 8:28-39

Does verse 28 say we *feel* that in all things God works for good? What does it say?

Has God called you to a purpose? What do you think your purpose is?

Did you know God knew you before time and already planned your life? Are you willing and listening for directions?

Read verse 30 – Did Jesus do the work?

What things can separate you from God?

Romans 9:1-29

Can you earn your way to heaven according to verses 11-12?

What does it depend on?

Do you have a hard heart towards Gods gift? What does God's gift of his son mean to you personally?

Is God molding you as a potter in verse 21?

Are you letting him mold you for his purposes or are you resisting and stiffening up when God is molding you? What makes molding so hard for you?

Romans 9:30-33

Are you pursuing by faith?

Are you pursuing by law?

Is it easier to work for something or is it easier to get it as a gift?

Do you have to work to receive salvation or is it a gift?

When you receive a gift, what is your attitude? Do you have the same attitude towards God and his gift?

Romans 10

What things are you zealous for?

Try putting verse 9 into memory. What does it mean for you to confess with your mouth? How about to believe in your heart?

What/who do you trust in?

How do we get faith according to verse 17?

Is God holding his hands out to you?

Romans 11:1-10

God knows you and knows your heart – will you ask him to show you who you are?

Do you feel alone when following God? A remnant is a small piece, what does it mean for you to be a part on his remnant?

Some eyes will not see and we do not know who they are – Do you have a willing heart and spirit to tell all those God puts in your path about his love and salvation and also his coming judgment?

Who do you need to tell?

Romans 11:11-24

Are you grafted in?

Are you amazed that God grafted you in? Why would he choose you?

Is God both kind and stern?

How do you remain in grafted?

Romans 11:33-36

Write down some things that stick out to you and mean something to you from this doxology? Why do they mean something to you?

Romans 12:1-8

How are you offering yourself to whatever God wants to use you for?

Where are you becoming like the world sometimes?

Where are you letting God transform you – are you giving him your thoughts?

What are your gifts?

Do you think you and your way of doing things are better than the person next to you?

Read verse 4 will you choose to give thanks for *each* person's gift? What gifts has God given your friends or family around you?

Romans 13

How important is it to submit and also to love? Find some verses here and write them down.

In looking at verse 11, when is the best time to believe and obey? Will you daily choose him?

Romans 14

Is it right to judge on disputable matters, what is a disputable matter?

Check out verse 5b – Are you convinced in your own mind or do you try to convince others minds in the disputable matters?

Will you stand before God and give an account for others or yourself?

What is the kingdom of God about?

According to verse 23 if you have doubts about a disputable matter should you do it or not do it and why or why not?

Romans 15:1-13

Write verse 1 out how it speaks to you personally.

How are you encouraging and bringing unity as you follow Christ at school, church, and home or at work?

Write out verse 13 and memorize it, turn it into a prayer for yourself. Maybe begin each day with it.

Romans 15:14-22

Who does your life bring glory to?

What is your goal in life spiritually and how do you work towards your goal in everyday life? Verse 20 was Paul's goal.

Do you thank God everyday for himself and giving you a desire to live for him? Will you live for him and not yourself today? What in your life needs to change to put him 1st?

Romans 15:23-33

Are you pleased to share whatever you have been given by the grace of God with others?

What have you been given that God could maybe ask you to share?

Do you pray for yourself and others each and everyday so God can work through you?

Where are you serving now? Have you begun it with prayer? "Prayer less service is powerless service."

Romans 16:1-16

Read this list of greetings – How are you greeting those God puts in your path?

How are you using words to thank your believing friends?

Does Paul love other believers – do you? Why is it hard at times?

Romans 16:17-27

What does Paul warn of?

Are you spending time in the truth so you can know what truth is?

How can you be wise about what is good and innocent about what is evil?

Who is able? Who gets the glory forever?

Do you know Christ personally and how are you living in his power?

I Corinthians 13

I Corinthians 13:3 – Are you sacrificing all you have but do not give any love? What do you gain?

Read and write down what love is.

Are you growing daily as in verses 11-12?

Scan the entire chapter – See which verses God draws your eyes and heart to and write them below.

II Corinthians 1:20-22

Did God place a seal on you – put his spirit in your heart and guaranteed what is to come? Are you excited or scared and why?

II Corinthians 2:14

What kind of fragrance or aroma are you?

II Corinthians 3:2–16

If you are a letter – what would others read and know about Christ through reading it?

Which verse speaks of a veil? What does that verse mean for you?

II Corinthians 4:7

Are you a clay pot showing Gods glory, or are you a pot with no cracks so no one can see what God has done or is doing in your life? Which one are you and why?

What are some of the cracks (trials) God has allowed in your life so others can see him and you can help others through your cracks?

II Corinthians 5:7

What is easier to live by faith or sight? Which one causes you to have peace?

II Corinthians 6:3-11

How have you experienced any of Paul's hardships?

How did Paul get in a position to have so many hardships?

II Corinthians 7:10

What does this verse mean to you?

Galatians 1

Find the verse that says what Jesus rescued you from in this world.

What gospel are some turning to?

Whose approval are you trying to win and are you a servant of Christ?

Where did Paul receive this gospel? Where do you receive your instruction?

Galatians 2:11-21

What was Peter doing in verses 12-13? Do you find yourself doing the same thing sometimes and why?

What do you do when you see others not living by the truth? What did Paul do?

Have you been crucified with Christ and striving to live in his power not your own?

Galatians 3

What are you relying on for salvation?

What were they relying on in verse 23?

According to verse 24 what is the law supposed to do?

What does the law mean to you?

Galatians 5

Does repentance bring freedom, how?

What does verse 6 say has value?

Read through the list of fruit. What is evident in your life? Which one do you wish would be easier?

Ephesians 6

Who are you serving?

Do you put your amour on daily?

Make a list of the amour you need from verse 10.

What is YOUR most important piece personally?

Philippians

Philippians 1:6 - Are you confident that Christ began a work in you and will finish it?

Philippians 4:8 - What is your mind on? What do you want it on?

Take some time to read all of Philippians – write down the verses that God points out.

Colossians 2:6-10

Have you received Christ as Lord (Lord meaning he controls you.)

How are you rooted and strengthened in Christ?

Is thankfulness a part of everyday life for you?

Is there danger to follow man and not Christ? What are ways this can happen?

Whose power are you submitting to?

I Thessalonians

Read it all slowly

1:2-3 - Who do you need to thank for telling you about Jesus? Will you do that this week?

4:11-12 - What is your ambition in life?

5:16 - Do you make this verse a habit? Do your circumstances determine how much joy you have?

II Thessalonians

Read it all slowly again

Is God just? What does it mean to be just?

1:8 - What will God do to those who do not know and obey him?

3:3 - Will God protect his children?

3:5 - Please pray for all those including yourself, that God will direct hearts into his love and Christ perseverance.

I Timothy

Read 2 and 3 and write down what is says about roles of us in worship.

4:7- How do you train yourself to be godly? Compare it to anything else you want to be good at...

6:7 - What do you take into this world? What do you take out of this world?

II Timothy 2:20-22

Are you set apart for noble purposes?

What evil desires do you need to flee? Is your heart seeking righteousness?

Are you looking for others on the same path to share the journey with? Who are they?

Titus

Chapter 2 - What should certain people teach and who should they teach?

3:4-5 - From what did God save you and why did he save you?

Philemon 1:6

How can you actively share your faith?

Who is your love refreshing? Whose love has refreshed you?

Hebrews 11

Which by faith story is meaningful to you and why?

What is your faith calling you to do? Don't think so big....

James

1:2 - In the trial or difficult circumstance you are in today – what is one thing you can be joyful about?

1:22-23 - If you are listening and not doing, what happens? What does God promise if you listen and obey?

2:13 - Who do you need to show mercy to today? What action will you take?

3:1-12 - What comes off your tongue?

4:10 - What does God want from you? Do you keep trying to do it all by yourself?

5:17-18 - What does your prayer life look like? What does it include, give me's or thank you's?

I Peter

1:23 - Is Gods word living and enduring in your life?

1:17 - How are you living as a stranger in this world?

5:10 - Have you lost hope – What is God's promise to you in this verse?

II Peter

1:3-4 - What has God given us to live here on earth?

2 - How do you know someone could be a false prophet?

3:11 - What kind of person should you be? What kind of person are you? Will you admit you need him and repent and turn from sin?

I John

1:8-10 - What do you do with your sin?

2:15 - How do you know you will live forever?

3:1 - Describe how this verse makes you feel?

4:4 - How does knowing God is greater than Satan, help you?

II John 6

Why do you think love is talked of so much?

Does love always "feel" good? Does love call us to be honest and speak God's truth?

What do you think of when you hear love?

III John 4

As a parent or a grandparent what is joy to them?

If you are not a parent/grandparent does your life bring joy to your parents/grandparents?

Do you have joy hearing others are walking in the truth? Are YOU walking in the truth?

Jude

Verses 20-21 - Is persevering easy?

How to you build yourself up?

Do you invite the Holy Spirit to pray you through?

What are you waiting for?

Revelation 22:7-21

Jesus is coming soon! How do you feel about that?

What will be your greatest reward? Are you still looking to get your reward here on earth or are you looking towards heaven?

Have you accepted the free gift of the water of life?

Printed in the United States
146352LV00003B/1/P